NATURE

This I-SPY book belongs to:_____

Introduction

The natural world around you is full of fascinating things to I-Spy. The planet on which we all live, Earth was created some 4500 million years ago. Such a vast span of time is impossible to imagine – it is roughly equivalent to sixty million human lifetimes! Over the ages, the planet has evolved and changed. At first there was no breathable air as we know it; there were no plants or animals, no blue sky. Now, millions of years later, there is a complex web of life; plants and animals, weather and rock are all part of the same great pattern. And remember, you are part of Nature too.

No single book could ever hope to include everything that you could spot but in I-Spy Nature, you will find all kinds of things – from clouds to rainbows, rocks and fossils to ice-cut valleys to flowering plants, insects to mammals – to look for. Go out and keep your eyes open. Look under stones (not forgetting to put them back) and up at the sky.

And don't forget, there is a lot to see in your garden.

But make sure you follow this simple rule: 'Take only photographs. Leave only footprints'

Take Care! There are poisonous plants and dangerous animals in the countryside. NEVER pick or eat any plant unless you are certain that it is good to eat. And watch out for dangerous animals that have a venomous bite or sting.

And remember; NEVER go out at night unless accompanied by a responsible adult.

How to use your I-SPY book

As you work through this book, you will notice that the subjects are arranged in groups which are related to the kinds of places where you are likely to find things. You need 1000 points to send off for your I-Spy certificate (see page 64) but that is not too difficult because there are masses of points in every book. As you make each I-Spy, write your score in the box and, where there is a question, double your score if you can answer it. Check your answer against the correct one on page 63.

CUMULUS

These are the best known 'cotton-wool' clouds which, when they are small and on their own in the sky, suggest that there is fair weather still to come.

I-SPY points: 5

Date: _____

CUMULONIMBUS

As banks of Cumulus clouds build up, they should be called Cumulonimbus, and as they darken, will eventually lead to rain.

I-SPY points: 10

Date: _____

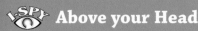

STRATOCUMULUS

These layered clouds often form as Cumulus clouds spread out across the sky. They may build up in thick, dark bands but usually lead only to showers.

I-SPY points: 15

Date: _____

ALTOCUMULUS

Altocumulus clouds form at high levels in the atmosphere. These clouds indicate that the high atmosphere is damp and unstable.

I-SPY points: 15

Date: _____

CIRRUS

The thin wispy streaks of Cirrus clouds are made up of ice particles and as they thicken, this suggests the approach of warm air, which may also lead to rain within 24 hours.

I-SPY points: 15

Date: _____

STORM CLOUDS

Cumulonimbus clouds can build up to form an anvil shape with blackening bases. These are storm clouds and are a sure sign of heavy rain to come.

I-SPY points: 10

Date: _____

RAINBOW

There is no 'pot of gold' at the end of the Rainbow. It is caused by droplets of water bending and splitting rays of light from the sun into the colours from which white light is made.

What are the seven colours of a rainbow?

I-SPY points: 15
Double with answer

Date: _____

RED SKY AT NIGHT

'Red sky at night, shepherds' delight'! This old saying is to some extent accurate: red suggests that there is good weather to come.

I-SPY points: 10

Date: _____

SNOWFLAKE

Everybody enjoys snow! It is beautiful to look at but can cause problems too. No two snowflakes are the same.

I-SPY points: 15

Date: _____

HAILSTONES

Hailstones are balls of ice that are formed high in the clouds. They are usually only a few millimetres in diameter, but can grow to 15cms and weigh 500gms. In these cases take cover!

I-SPY points: 15

Date: _____

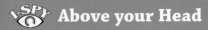

COMMON PIPISTRELLE

This tiny bat roosts in cracks in buildings and trees. It feeds on small flying insects which it hunts for over woodland, farmland, and moorland.

I-SPY points: 30

Date: _____

DAUBENTON'S BAT

About a quarter of the world's mammals are bats. This bat can be seen in the evening skimming over water chasing flies.

True or False - Bats will get caught in your hair?

I-SPY points: 30
Double with answer

Date: _____

MUTE SWAN

This is one of the birds that we all enjoy feeding at the pond but watch out; they can get aggressive when they have a brood of cygnets (young swans).

I-SPY points: 10

Date: _____

MAGPIE

A common member of the crow family, magpies are black and white with a long tail. Their nest is a large ball of twigs, often found in a roadside bush.

I-SPY points: 10

Date: _____

HOUSE SPARROW

These cheeky sparrows are often seen dust bathing in flower beds or at the side of the road. They will happily eat crumbs and seeds from a bird table.

I-SPY points: 10

Date: _____

STARLING

In spring, if you hear a noise in your attic, it's likely to be a nest of starlings. They have been known to mimic sounds from their surroundings.

I-SPY points: 10

Date: _____

10

BLUE TIT

Their acrobatics on bird feeders fill us with admiration and these colourful birds are also the gardener's friend, as they eat lots of insect pests.

I-SPY points: 5

Date: _____

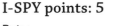

BLACKBIRD

The male blackbird in spring is truly handsome with his shiny black plumage and yellow beak. His melodious song signifies that winter is over at last.

I-SPY points: 5

Date: _____

MALLARD

The mallard is our most abundant wild duck and is a familiar bird to most people.

I-SPY points: 5

Date: _____

CANADA GEESE

Introduced into Europe more than 200 years ago, they are now native and can be seen in large flocks on lakes, park ponds or in the fields cropping grass.

I-SPY points: 10

Date: _____

ROBIN

Both male and female robin have the red breast and are almost impossible to tell apart. It doesn't matter, we love them both.

I-SPY points: 5

Date: _____

COMMON HAZEL

Hazel has been coppiced for centuries. The resulting poles provide firewood, hurdles and thatching spars. The familiar nuts are eaten by a wide variety of creatures, including us.

I-SPY points: 10

Date: _____

APPLE

All modern day apple trees are descended from the wild crab apple. Domestic apple trees usually need a companion tree to pollinate them and then they can then bear edible fruit.

I-SPY points: 5

Date: _____

PEAR

Pear trees grow up to 17m in height and are thought to have originated in China where they have been grown for at least 3,000 years. Pear wood is often used in the manufacture of musical instruments.

I-SPY points: 10

Date: _____

CHERRY

The cultivation of cherries died out in England during the middle-ages but luckily, this healthy fruit was re-introduced by Henry VIII. Look for the pink flowers in May.

I-SPY points: 10

Date: _____

14

SYCAMORE

A deciduous member of the maple family that can grow to 35m tall. It most notable feature however, is the keyed seeds.

I-SPY points: 15

Date: _____

COMMON YEW

This strong but springy wood was the best for making longbows. In more modern times it has been found that the leaves contain an effective anti-cancer treatment.

I-SPY points: 15

Date: _____

ENGLISH OAK

The oak is viewed as a symbol of strength and longevity. It is also very important to insects and other wildlife. Jays are responsible for planting more oak trees than humans!

I-SPY points: 10

Date:

HORSE CHESTNUT

In spring the tree is covered with stunning white "candles" and in the autumn there will be a crop of nuts which can be used to play conkers.

I-SPY points: 5

Date:

COMMON HAWTHORN

Farmers appreciate this tree because it forms an impenetrable thorny hedge, ideal for containing animals. Its bright red berries provide colour during autumn and winter.

I-SPY points: 15

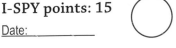

Date: _____

HOLLY

To us the red berries on the holly mean one thing - Christmas! To wildlife, they can make the difference between surviving winter or not.

I-SPY points: 5

Date: _____

SILVER BIRCH

The silver birch is a beautiful tree that has long been associated with the start of new life, due to its outstanding ability to colonise newly cleared land quickly.

I-SPY points: 10

Date: _____

LEYLAND CYPRUS

This tree is more commonly known as Leylandii and is often used as hedges. If not clipped it can reach heights of up to 30m.

I-SPY points: 5

Date: _____

BLACKTHORN

This tree is covered in long, vicious "black thorns". It heralds the arrival of warmer weather by covering itself in white blossom. The fruit of the blackthorn is a small plum called a Sloe.

I-SPY points: 10

Date:_____

ELDER

The elder is usually not much more than a bush. But it is versatile; it feeds birds and animals, the bark and flowers can make dyes and last but not least, a twig can make a good fishing float!

I-SPY points: 15

Date:_____

PRIMROSE

A true harbinger of spring, what could be nicer than driving down a country lane flanked by these beautiful pale yellow flowers.

I-SPY points: 10

Date: _____

COMMON DANDELION

The scourge of gardeners but beneficial to insects, the root of this plant has long been used by herbalists to stimulate the digestive system.

I-SPY points: 5

Date: _____

RED CAMPION

A tall plant that produces pink flowers on long stems in May and June. Bumble bees bite through the base of the plant to reach the store of nectar.

I-SPY points: 15

Date: _____

COMMON POPPY

This common plant appeared by their millions in the battlefields after the First World War, and has been adopted as a symbol of peace and remembrance ever since.

I-SPY points: 10

Date: _____

RAGWORT

It is thought that steam trains helped to spread the seeds of this plant as they rushed by. Not good news for horses; ragwort is harmful if mixed with dried grasses and hay as feed.

I-SPY points: 10

Date: _____

COMMON GORSE

Gorse bushes flower in most months of the year. Their coconut scented flowers are beneficial to honey bees and other pollinators. A delicious wine can be made from the yellow petals.

I-SPY points: 15

Date: _____

CREEPING BUTTERCUP

Its creeping habit will swamp all other plants and although pretty, it's actually poisonous and gloves should be worn when weeding.

I-SPY points: 10

Date:

YELLOW IRIS

The roots or rhizomes of this waterside plant used to be crushed and the resulting juice used to make a black dye or ink.

I-SPY points: 10

Date:

THRIFT

The name refers to its ability to flourish on rocky sea cliffs with very little fresh water or soil, all the while being subjected to wind and salt spray.

I-SPY points: 15

Date: _____

SPEAR THISTLE

Since 1503, the thistle has been the symbol of Scotland. Its biennial habit makes it unpopular with gardeners but the large (40mm) flowers are much sought after by butterflies and bees.

I-SPY points: 10

Date: _____

DOG ROSE

The symbol of the British monarchy is a good source of vitamin C. The bright red hips can be made into Rose Hip Syrup.

I-SPY points: 10

Date: _____

BRAMBLE

If you brave the straggly thorns, you will enjoy the pleasures of blackberrying! And the apple and blackberry pie that follows!

I-SPY points: 5

Date: _____

IVY

Ivy gives so much: late season nectar for butterflies, for birds it offers a place to build a nest, hide from predators and provides food from its berries.

I-SPY points: 5
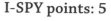
Date: _____

COMMON DUCKWEED

Duckweed is a strange but very valuable habitat; water-borne insects shelter beneath it, up above it's a staple diet of many water birds.

I-SPY points: 10

Date: _____

GROUND ELDER

The gardener's enemy brought here by the Romans as a herbal medicine; it's not going home any time soon so we might as well live with it and its pretty white flowers.

I-SPY points: 5

Date: _____

COMMON NETTLE

Apart from the obvious sting, this is a really versatile plant; it can be eaten, infused and provide relieve from chest complaints.

I-SPY points: 5

Date: _____

ADDER

Britain's only poisonous snake is shy and will glide silently away if at all possible. Seek urgent anti-venom treatment from hospital if bitten!

I-SPY points: 30

Date: _____

GRASS SNAKE

Grass snakes may grow to 1m in length. They live in grassy areas near rivers, ditches and streams and they are excellent swimmers. They do not have a venomous bite, but can still be scary!

I-SPY points: 25

Date: _____

STOAT

You can tell the playful and inquisitive stoat from the smaller weasel by the black tip it has at the end of its tail.

I-SPY points: 20

Date: _____

WEASEL

A small (up to 23cm excluding tail) but ferocious brown and white hunter. They need to eat a third of their own body weight every day.

I-SPY points: 20

Date: _____

PINE MARTIN

They are becoming more common thanks to conservationists and have even been known to live in attics and feed at bird tables.

I-SPY points: 20

Date: _____

FERN

Ferns need rich, damp soil to thrive and this is why they love the woodland floor where they enjoy the shade.

I-SPY points: 15

Date: _____

LICHEN

The 17,000 species of Lichens are not actually plants at all but a partnership between a fungus and algae. Some colonies may be 9,000 years old.

I-SPY points: 15

Date: _____

AMMONITE

Anyone who has visited the beach at Lyme Regis in Dorset will be familiar with these fossils. The animals are extinct but they are related to modern squids and octopuses.

I-SPY points: 10

Date: _____

BELEMNITE

These fossils are also related to octopuses and squids but the bullet shaped fossil is similar in many ways to the internal skeleton of a cuttlefish.

I-SPY points: 10

Date: _____

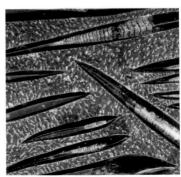

TRILOBITE

A trilobite is an arthropod – an animal with jointed legs like an insect or a spider. Fossils of this animal are found in rocks more than 400 million years old.

I-SPY points: 15

Date: _____

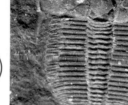

GRAPTOLITE

This fossil's name means 'stone writing' because when it was first discovered, this is what scientists thought the fossils looked like. This one is at least 400 million years old.

I-SPY points: 20

Date: _____

SEA URCHIN

This is the 'skeleton', preserved as a chalky fossil of a sea urchin or echinoid called Nucleolites (pronounced 'new clee-oh-lie-teas') which lived on the sea bottom more than 120 million years ago.

I-SPY points: 15

Date: _____

SANDY BEACH

This kind of broad, gently sloping sandy beach occurs where the swell from the open sea rolls in, deposits some sand and pulls much of it back into the sea again.

I-SPY points: 10

Date: _____

BOULDER BEACH

When rocks are continuously washed to and fro in the water, the sharp edges are gradually worn away and they become rounded. This can take millions of years.

I-SPY points: 15

Date: _____

ROCKY SHORE

The cliffs and fallen rocks beneath are made from a rock called sandstone which in this case, was formed some 250 million years ago.

I-SPY points: 10

Date: _____

WHITE CLIFFS

These white sea cliffs are made from a rock called chalk. It was formed from the skeletons of many billions of tiny animals which lived almost 100 million years ago. The cliffs are constantly eroded when pounded by the sea.

I-SPY points: 10

Date: _____

SEA ARCH

A sea arch forms where the action
of the waves hollows out a cave
on either side of a headland.
Eventually the two caves meet and
the arch is made.

I-SPY points: 15

Date:

WAVE-CUT PLATFORM

These are formed at the base of
a cliff, sometimes by the erosive
action of the waves, but landward
erosion by freshwater is also
sometimes to blame.

I-SPY points: 15

Date:

SAND DUNES

These hills of sand, build up behind sandy beaches where dry sand is blown and trapped by plants such as Marram Grass. Dunes form a natural land defence from the sea.

I-SPY points: 15

Date: _____

SHINGLE BAR

When waves approach the coast at an angle, sand and shingle are washed along the shore; this is called long-shore drift.

What do we use to prevent the effects of long-shore drift?

I-SPY points: 20
Double with answer

Date: _____

FOLDED ROCKS

Here you can clearly see how the layers of rocks, from which the land is made, have been folded by forces within the earth's crust.

I-SPY points: 20

Date: _____

SCHIST

Look at this rock exposed in a sea cliff. It seems to glisten in the sunlight. It is mineral called mica that gives this layered rock its shine.

I-SPY points: 20

Date: _____

MARRAM GRASS

You will find this tough grass doing a great job by the sea; it builds sand dunes and protects our coasts from erosion.

I-SPY points: 10

Date: _____

STACK

A stack is formed from an arch, after the continuous erosion by the sea eventually causes it to collapse leaving the seaward pillar of the arch isolated.

I-SPY points: 20

Date: _____

RAISED BEACH

If you look towards the top of some beaches, you will see that it is made of a shingly or sandy material. This was once the beach and now the sea level has fallen in relation to the land.

I-SPY points: 25

Date: _____

WORM CAST

The coils of compacted mud or sand are made by worms living beneath, which pass them out as they extract food from beach material.

I-SPY points: 15

Date: _____

STARFISH

Among the creatures that you can find at the shore, a starfish is one of the most exciting. If a starfish loses one of its arms, it can simply grow another one.

I-SPY points: 20

Date: _____

BLADDER WRACK

Bladder wrack is actually a type of algae. Wrack is a general name given to certain kinds of brown seaweeds.

Do you know why it is called bladder wrack?

I-SPY points: 10

Double with answer

Date: _____

FAULT

Rocks do not always fold when pulled or pushed by the earth's forces. When they break they are called faults.

I-SPY points: 20

Date: _____

40

GREY SEAL

They are inquisitive creatures and will swim with divers given the chance. Grey seals are much larger than the common seal.

I-SPY points: 20

Date: _____

COMMON SEAL

From a distance, they look like dogs in the water and are most easily seen on the east coast.

I-SPY points: 15

Date: _____

FIREBREAK

Heaths and forests can become very dry in summer so there is always a risk of fire. Workers cut wide channels through vulnerable land to prevent fire spreading and often use them as tracks.

I-SPY points: 15

Date:

I-SPY points: 15

Date:

U-SHAPED VALLEY

These valleys were carved into a smooth U-shape by glaciers. You will also see large boulders left by the retreating ice.

42

MOUNTAINS

Mountains are higher than hills, usually more rugged and rocky and notably higher than the land around. The higher the land, the less vegetation grows.

I-SPY points: 10

Date: _____

I-SPY points: 15

Date: _____

HEATHLAND

Heath and moorland are types of countryside where the majority of plants grow on acid soils.

CAIRNS

Cairns are piles of small flat stones placed on mountain paths, they help travellers stay on the right path and show them the way.

I-SPY points: 10

Date: _____

GRANITE

Granite is an igneous rock (formed by fire). The granite outcrops called Tors have been exposed by erosion of their surrounding soil.

I-SPY points: 15

Date: _____

ROCHE MOUTONNEE

Pronounced 'rosh moo-tonn-ay', this is a rock which has been smoothed and rounded by a glacier passing over it.

I-SPY points: 25

Date:

MOUNTAIN STREAM

When rivers are close to their source in steeply graded land, they tumble through deep, V-shaped valleys.

I-SPY points: 10

Date:

LIMESTONE PAVEMENT

Limestone is a rock that can be dissolved by acid. Rainwater is slightly acid and where the rock is exposed, the rainwater opens up the natural joints in the rock by dissolving it away.

I-SPY points: 15

Date:

I-SPY points: 15

Date:

DRYSTONE WALLING

In some areas, such as the Yorkshire Dales, limestone rocks are used to make walls without mortar to hold them together. The bare hillsides seem to have a 'net' of walls diving it up in to curiously shaped fields. To make these walls is a special skill.

HEATHER

With its mauve flowers, heather is a low-growing shrub that grows on heath and moorland. It is often managed by controlled burning to clear the land.

I-SPY points: 10

Date: _____

COTTON-GRASS

During May and June, the seed heads of this sedge are covered in a fluffy mass of cotton which is carried on the wind.

I-SPY points: 15

Date: _____

WATERFALL

A waterfall forms where there is softer rock downstream from harder rock.

Which is the world's highest waterfall?

I-SPY points: 15

Double with answer

Date: _____

MEANDER

In a flat valley floor where the gradient is shallow, a river will flow by swinging from side to side in a series of curves called meanders. This has formed over thousands of years.

I-SPY points: 15

Date: _____

48

BULRUSH

The bulrush can easily be recognised by its female flower which looks like a brown sausage right at the top of a 200cm stalk.

I-SPY points: 10

Date: _____

COMMON REED

Millions of starlings use it as a winter roost. During the breeding season countless other birds, either nest in it, or use its leaves and stems to construct their nests.

I-SPY points: 10

Date: _____

COMMON FROG

The frog has a smooth skin and varies in colour from green to yellow. It will live anywhere that is damp but it lays its eggs in ponds.

I-SPY points: 15

Date:

COMMON TOAD

Like frogs, toads also breed in ponds. They are larger than frogs with shorter hind legs and a warty skin.

To what group of animals do frogs and toads belong?

I-SPY points: 15

Double with answer

Date:

SMOOTH NEWT

Newts emerge from hibernation and head to freshwater to breed. Newts are carnivorous (meat eaters) throughout their life.

I-SPY points: 20

Date:

OTTER

The otter is largely nocturnal and secretive due to past persecution. A wildlife sanctuary is the best place to see one.

I-SPY points: 20

Date: _____

I-SPY points: 15

Date: _____

MINK

Originally introduced into Britain to be bred for its fur, the mink has been released by activists into the wild and is now a major predator of birds, fish and other aquatic life.

FOX

Foxes are surprisingly common mammals and they now find their way into towns and gardens and will even raid dustbins for food, especially at night.

I-SPY points: 20

Date: _____

BADGER

Sadly, you are most likely to see a dead badger killed on the road. But, if you find a sett, you might be able to see one emerge from its entrance at dusk if you stay very still and upwind of the animal.

I-SPY points: 50

Date: _____

MOLE

A mole spends almost all of its life underground. You will be very lucky to see a live one above ground, but you can easily find evidence of them from the mole hills they leave behind.

What do moles usually eat?

I-SPY a mole hill points: 10
Double with answer

Date: _____

52

BROWN RAT

An intelligent animal but a serious pest and health hazard; rats destroy millions of tonnes of food around the world every year and can be found almost anywhere.

I-SPY points: 15

<u>Date:</u>

WOOD MOUSE

This is the probably the creature that you can hear scrabbling about in the corner of a bike shed or even in your attic.

I-SPY points: 10

<u>Date:</u>

SHORT-TAILED VOLE

This is one of Europe's most common mammals; it moves about using shallow tunnels in grasslands. Their population fluctuates in a four-year cycle.

I-SPY points: 20

<u>Date:</u>

GREY SQUIRREL

An engaging pest; they strip the bark of young trees, eat the young and eggs of songbirds and carries the squirrel pox virus to our native red squirrel.

I-SPY points: 5

Date: _____

RED SQUIRREL

Cute and rare, now unfortunately only seen in a few isolated places.

I-SPY points: 25

Date: _____

MUNTJAC

This small deer was released into the wild in 1921, since then it has spread throughout the British Isles.

I-SPY points: 20

Date: _____

FALLOW DEER

If you see a deer, it is most likely to be a Fallow Deer. One of our native deer, it has been around for 400,000 years but was almost hunted to extinction in the 14th century.

I-SPY points: 15

Date: _____

HEDGEHOG

Hedgehogs are active mainly at night and you can sometimes hear them snuffling around a garden. They are good swimmers and surprisingly agile climbers. Their spikes are there for protection.

I-SPY points: 15

Date: _____

BROWN HARE

At first glance a hare looks a little like a rabbit, but it's actually bigger with longer ears and legs. In spring, pairs or even groups can sometimes be seen boxing with one another.

I-SPY points: 20

Date: _____

RABBIT

You'll find rabbits in most of the countryside where there is plant food for them to eat and suitable places for them to make their burrows.

I-SPY points: 5

Date: _____

DRAGONFLY

Dragonflies are identified by two pairs of transparent wings and an elongated body. They are normally found around lakes, ponds and streams.

I-SPY points: 10

Date:

DAMSELFLY

Similar to the Dragonfly, you can tell them apart as the wings of most damselflies are positioned parallel to the body when at rest. They are usually smaller and poorer fliers than dragonflies.

I-SPY points: 15

Date:

HOVERFLY

Although hoverflies resemble wasps, they do not sting. They do however eat huge numbers of aphids and are of great benefit to farmers and gardeners.

I-SPY points: 10

Date:

HONEY BEE

A bee colony may contain 60,000 individual insects, all controlled by the queen.

I-SPY points: 10

Date: _____

BUMBLE BEE

To hear the buzzing of this large, gentle but ungainly bee is to hear the sound of summer.

I-SPY points: 10

Date: _____

COMMON WASP

The common wasp can be annoying on picnics, but is useful for the gardener as it feeds on aphids and other garden pests.

I-SPY points: 5

Date: _____

STAG BEETLE

A most impressive insect at over 40mm long plus the horns! Its larvae live in rotting tree stumps. In summer they emerge as adult beetles.

I-SPY points: 20

Date: _____

HOUSE SPIDER

The house spider won't harm you, so don't be frightened and leave it alone in a corner of your room and it will help to keep your house free of flies and bugs all summer long.

I-SPY points: 5

Date: _____

MONEY SPIDER

This tiny spider has been revered as a good luck charm since Roman times. They can travel great distances by spinning a silk parachute and floating on the wind.

I-SPY points: 15

Date: _____

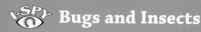

SANDHOPPER

It lives under rotting seaweed or deep in sand. When disturbed it will jump several centimetres to escape.

I-SPY points: 15

Date:

LADYBIRD

Everyone likes this colourful insect. There are more than 40 species, they all have spots and some can give you a small bite if annoyed!

I-SPY points: 10

Date:

RED ADMIRAL

This large, brightly coloured butterfly is usually first seen in May or June but, although it is a Mediterranean insect, some individuals do manage to survive the harsh British winter.

I-SPY points: 15

Date: _____

PEACOCK

This large, brightly coloured insect may be seen during April and May and then again in September and October.

I-SPY points: 15

Date: _____

COMMA

The comma has tattered looking wings for camouflage but it is the pale comma-shaped markings on the underwings, which give this butterfly its name.

I-SPY points: 15

Date: _____

EMPEROR

The Emperor moth is common over much of Britain, you are most likely to find one on moorland and open country.

I-SPY points: 20

Date: _____

BROWN HOUSE

One of two common species of moth found in our homes, the other being the slightly smaller white-shouldered house moth. Their caterpillars feed on crumbs and other bits of food that collect around our houses.

I-SPY points: 10

Date: _____

LARGE ELEPHANT HAWK MOTH

This very beautiful moth is fairly common and may be found from May onwards, quite often in gardens. The small elephant hawk is similar but with less pink on the wings.

I-SPY points: 25

Date: _____

Index

First published by Michelin Maps and Guides 2009
© Michelin, Proprietaires-Editeurs 2009.
Michelin and the Michelin Man are registered
Trademarks of Michelin.
Created and produced by Blue Sky Publishing Limited.
All rights reserved. No part of this publication may be
reproduced, copied or transmitted in any form without
the prior consent of the publisher.
Printed in China.
The publisher gratefully acknowledges the contribution
of the I-Spy team: Camilla Lovell, Graeme Newton-Cox,
Ruth Neilson and Trey Watts in the production of this title.
The publisher gratefully acknowledges the contribution
of David Fenwick who provided the majority of the
photographs in this I-Spy book. The publisher also
gratefully acknowledges the co-operation and assistance
of the following who supplied pictures for this title: Melvin
Grey, Andrew Francis, Anthony Dixon, Jim Woods, John
Harvey, Terry Gunby, Trevor Gunby, Shirley Roulston,
Bill Deer and Unitaw Limited. Other images in the public
domain and used under a creative commons licence.
Reprinted 2011   10 9 8 7

Answers: P6 Rainbow: Violet, Indigo, Blue, Green, Yellow, Orange, Red. **P8** Daubenton's Bat: False. **P36** Shingle Bar: Groynes. **P40** Bladder Wrack: Because of the air bladders which make its fronds (leaves) float. **P48** Waterfall: Angel Falls in Venezuela 979m (3,212ft). **P50** Toad: Amphibians **P52** Mole: Worms

HOW TO GET YOUR I-SPY CERTIFICATE AND BADGE

Every time you score 1000 points or more in an I-Spy book, you can apply for a certificate

Here's what to do, step by step:

Certificate

- Ask an adult to check your score
- Ask his or her permission to apply for a certificate
- Apply online to www.ispymichelin.com
- Enter your name and address and the completed title
- We will send you back via e mail your certificate for the title

Badge

- Each I-Spy title has a cut out (page corner) token at the back of the book
- Collect five tokens from different I-Spy titles
- Put Second Class Stamps on two strong envelopes
- Write your own address on one envelope and put a £1 coin inside it (for protection). Fold, but do not seal the envelope, and place it inside the second envelope
- Write the following address on the second envelope, seal it carefully and post to:

I-Spy Books
Michelin Maps and Guides
Hannay House
39 Clarendon Road
Watford
WD17 1JA

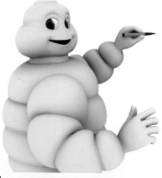